Women And The Word

Ten Narratives On God's Word

Kris Linner

CSS Publishing Company, Inc., Lima, Ohio

WOMEN AND THE WORD

Copyright © 2007 by
CSS Publishing Company, Inc.
Lima, Ohio

Scripture quotations are from the Revised Standard Version of the Bible, copyrighted 1946, 1952 ©, 1971, 1973, by the Division of Christian Education of the National Council of the Churches of Christ in the USA. Used by permission.

Library of Congress Cataloging-in-Publication Data

Linner, Kris, 1958-
    Women and the word : ten narratives on God's word / Kris Linner.
    p. cm.
    ISBN 0-7880-2446-9 (perfect bound : alk. paper)
  1. Women in the Bible. 2. Bible stories, English. I. Title.

BS575.L54 2007
226'.0922082—dc22

2006036022

For more information about CSS Publishing Company resources, visit our website at www.csspub.com or email us at custserv@csspub.com or call (800) 241-4056.

Cover design by Perry Hodies III and Barbara Spencer
ISBN-13: 978-0-7880-2446-7
ISBN-10: 0-7880-2446-9   PRINTED IN U.S.A.

*Dedicated to all the women
who have lived God's Word into my life,
especially
my grandmother, Kristine,
my mother, Evie,
and
my daughters, Greta and Tina*

Table Of Contents

Listen to the words of a petrified teenage girl. She has an amazing encounter with a member of the heavenly host that completely changes the course of her life ... forever! Mary, Joseph's betrothed, learns that the promise the angel gives to her — With God, all things are possible — will sustain her not only through the birth, but also throughout the life of her son, who is the Savior of the world.

A Promised Word
Luke 1:26-38

I was doing housework and daydreaming about being married to Joseph, the man my parents had arranged for me to marry. I wondered what was in store for my future with Joseph. He seemed like a nice enough man; gentle, honorable, and hard-working. I thought he would make a good husband, but I just could not picture what it would be like to be married at such a young age. So, in the midst of an unknown future, I spent a great deal of time daydreaming and praying.

Then right in the middle of my prayer, while sweeping the floor, I heard someone talking. I turned around to see who was at the door, but no one was there. Then I heard it again, a soft, gentle voice saying, "Hail." I looked up and could not believe my eyes. I thought I was seeing things. It looked like an angel but, I knew it couldn't be. I had not been sleeping well, so I assumed that because I was overtired my mind was playing tricks on me. I shook it off and went back to my chores. Then I heard it again. "Hail, O favored one! The Lord is with you."

Now that certainly sounded like the greeting of an angel, but I did not think an angel would be speaking to me that way. Why would I be favored? I was only a poor teenager. I think of God's favored ones as the rabbis or the Pharisees. Certainly, God doesn't favor poor, lowly girls. Then I heard it again. "Hail, O favored one! The Lord is with you."

I said, "Who me?"

"Yes, you are favored. The Lord is with you."

I was terrified. Absolutely terrified. I was shaking with fear. I felt confused and wondered why the angel was talking to me and what the greeting could possibly mean.

I am sure you know that feeling of terror. I think that each of you can remember a time when you have felt afraid, confused, or perplexed. Maybe it was when the doctor said the word, "cancer." Or it might have been when you saw your loved one die. It could have been when your partner said, "I just don't love you anymore." For some it might have been facing an unknown future. You know what I am talking about when I say that I was absolutely terrified, don't you?

Well, the angel sensed my fear and said very gently, "Do not be afraid, Mary." It was then that I realized that the angel was a messenger of the Lord. Those were words God spoke frequently to God's people. God spoke them to Abraham when Abraham feared he would have no offspring. Moses heard those words when he feared the daunting task of facing Pharaoh. God shared the words, "Do not fear or be dismayed," with Joshua before sending him into battle. An angel of the Lord calmed Gideon when he feared for his life. Isaiah, Jeremiah, and the other prophets needed a great deal of reassurance and God frequently encouraged them by saying, "Fear not, for I am with you." That is how I knew that Gabriel was a messenger of the Lord. "Do not fear," are God's words of promise for God's people. They hold the promise that God always goes with us. With God's presence we have nothing to fear.

Gabriel's assuring words calmed me. But then he went on with words that confused me. Gabriel said, "You have found favor with God," which made me wonder. Why should I, a poor teenager, find favor with God? Why not a priest? Why not a prophet? My faith seemed pretty ordinary to me, but it certainly was not noteworthy enough that it would warrant God's favor. That much I knew.

As I was trying to figure out what in the world Gabriel could have meant, he went on to say, "You will conceive in your womb and bear a son, and you will name him Jesus." My eyes must have been as big as saucers. I could not believe what I was hearing. How could I bear a son? The impossible announcement was more than I could comprehend, but the angel quickly went on saying, "He will be great, and will be called the Son of the Most High, and the Lord God will give to him the throne of his ancestor David. He will reign over the house of Jacob forever, and of his kingdom there will be no end."

I thought I was confused before, but after that announcement my head was swirling. As a teenager my emotions were already beyond control. I felt panicked. What would my friends think? How would I deal with my parents? Would Joseph dump me or maybe even have me stoned to death? How could I be the mother of the Son of the Most High? I could not make sense of any of it. So I just point blankly asked Gabriel, "What do you mean? How could this be? I am not even married."

Gabriel went on to explain that it would all be done by the power of the Most High. Let me tell you, I was a bit skeptical about that until the angel told me about my elderly relative, Elizabeth, who was six months pregnant. Elizabeth had so wanted children and had never been able to have them. Elizabeth and her husband were old, *way* too old to have children, yet she was pregnant.

Thinking that Elizabeth was pregnant in her old age made me believe the angel's words of promise, "For with God nothing will be impossible." Clinging to the promise that *nothing*, absolutely nothing, is impossible with God gave me the courage to respond by saying, "Here am I, servant of the Lord; let it be with me according to your word."

I trusted that God would be with me regardless of what happened. I believed that God was with me so I had nothing to fear. I knew that with God's strength I could face any challenge. I knew that God's power could change me and change the world forever through the birth of Jesus.

You know the rest of my story. You have been hearing it all of your lives. I ran as fast as I could to see Elizabeth, because I knew she would believe me. I knew she would believe all that Gabriel had told me. I know she would trust in God's promised Word.

Nine months later, while Joseph and I were in Bethlehem for the census, it came time for me to give birth. I was frightened. There was no room for us in the inn. There was no one to help us. Our parents were not there. There was not even a midwife. As the contractions got closer, I wondered if Joseph would know what to do. It felt like my world was spinning out of control. Joseph left me to find a place to stay. It felt like he was gone for hours. Upon his return he told me that the only place he could find was a stable. There was no time to complain, the baby was coming. I was terrified, but I clung to God's promise of old, "Fear not for I am with you." Once again those words of promise calmed my fears and gave me comfort.

God's promised Word brought Joseph and I through the ordeal of childbirth.

As I held Jesus in my arms for the first time and looked in his eyes I thought, "With God nothing is impossible." Giving birth in a stable without a midwife was the first of many challenges throughout my life. At times, I felt anything but blessed. There were times when I watched my son go through the ups and downs of childhood, the challenges of ministry and finally his being mocked, spit upon, ridiculed, and finally crucified. My soul was pierced as I watched the son, to whom I'd given birth, die on a cross.

However, through all the ups and downs I trusted God and I always came back to the promises that God spoke to me as a teenage girl. I trusted that there was nothing to fear because I was not alone. I believed that God's plan for salvation was revealed through my son, Jesus, and his kingdom would have no end. I trusted the promise: with God nothing is impossible.

Those promises that Gabriel spoke to me so long ago are promises for you today. You know as well as I do that God did not promise any of us a life of ease. As blessed children of God we are not exempt from hardship. Disease still drains the life out of loved ones. Loneliness robs people of joy. Death rips hearts with grief. Personal crises strip away emotional fortitude. Physical pain invades life's comfort.

Yet, you can cling to the promises that helped me through my life. There is nothing to fear because God is with you. That is why God sent my son, Jesus, into the world. In a dream, my husband was told to name our son "Emmanuel" which means "God-with-us." God is for you. God loves you. God is with you. That is the promise that can wash away any fear.

But that is not all. My son was the promised Messiah, the Savior of the world. That was the promise that the angels spoke to the shepherds the night I gave birth. "For unto you is born this day in the city of David, a Savior who is Christ the Lord." There is nothing that can separate you from God's love known through Jesus. Sin can't. Actions can't. Words can't. Thoughts can't. Not even death can separate you from the love of God, because with God nothing is impossible.

That is what will get you through anything in life. You have nothing to fear because Jesus, your Savior, whose kingdom will have no end, will be with you always. You can get through any hardship that life brings because with God all things are possible. Those words of promise worked for me and they will work for you as well. Have no fear, because God is with you and with God *nothing* is impossible.

Listen to the words of a woman of the city. She cowers in shame, for all who pass by know how she makes her living. She watches from the sidelines, hoping always that someone will love her and care about her. When she finally encounters Jesus, she is transformed. Though still misunderstood by the religious leaders, she knows that people who are forgiven much sin are people who love very deeply.

A Forgiving Word
Luke 7:36-50

As a woman of the city, I studied people. People intrigued me; the powerful and the powerless, the righteous and the sinful, the rich and the poor. I saw it all. I watched those who pursued power like a vicious predator and those who gave up power for the sake of love. I watched those who made themselves feel good by stepping on others and those who built others up because they knew what it was like to be stepped on. Watching people was an interesting way for me to pass the time, but there was one person who really captured my attention. It was Jesus.

There was something different about him. His words matched his actions. He talked a lot about loving others and he did it. He loved people and not just the people that were deserving of love. In fact, he went out of his way to love people others considered to be unlovable.

One day I heard him tell the story of a Good Samaritan, a man who stopped and helped a man who had been beaten and left for dead. Jesus told those listening that there were religious leaders who ignored the man's need and walked by. I remember thinking that Jesus was a Good Samaritan. I never saw him walk past anyone in need. He did not ignore the blind beggar nor did he walk by the lame leper. Jesus, like the Good Samaritan, did the loving thing. He always stopped with loving concern to help those in need.

I wanted to hear more of what he was saying so I followed the crowd to where Jesus was speaking. The crowd was huge. It was so huge that some people carrying a paralyzed man could not get close to Jesus, so they lowered him through the roof. When Jesus saw the faith of the man's friends he said, "Your sins are forgiven." Well, that got the Pharisees in an uproar. They started shouting, "Who is this that speaks blasphemies? Who can forgive sins but

God only?" Jesus' response amazed me. He said, "Why do you question in your hearts? Which is easier, to say, 'Your sins are forgiven you,' or to say 'Rise and walk'? But that you may know that the son of man has authority on earth to forgiven sins" — he said to the man who was paralyzed — "I say to you, rise, take up your bed and go home." And he did! The man walked away.

Everyone was filled with awe and I was filled with hope. I was desperately hopeful that the words spoken to the paralyzed man were words that Jesus would speak to me as well. I needed to hear those words, "Your sins are forgiven," because I no longer believed that anyone could forgive me, especially God.

So, I continued to listen to Jesus any time I had the chance. I would often work my way to the front of the crowd hoping that Jesus would see the heavy burden of unforgiven sin which I carried as my constant companion.

Then one day, I watched Jesus interact with a woman caught in adultery. What was strange to me was that the Scribes and Pharisees that brought her before Jesus did not bring the man who was also caught in adultery. Where was he? Doesn't adultery take two? It seems that they were trying to trap Jesus when they said, "Teacher, this woman has been caught in the act of adultery. Now, in the law, Moses commanded us to stone such. What do you say about her?" Jesus did not respond for a long time as he was writing something in the sand.

Then he said, "Let him who is without sin among you be the first to throw a stone at her." While Jesus bent down and wrote in the sand the self-righteous accusers went away. But, I stayed close. I wanted to hear what he would say. I needed to hear how he responded to the accused woman. He looked at her with great gentleness and said, "Woman, where are they? Has no one condemned you?" She said, "No one, Lord." And Jesus said, "Neither do I condemn you; go, and do not sin again." Then he turned to me with the same gentle, loving look and nodded to me.

I knew in my heart that he had also said those words to me. Everyone that I met on the street gave me a look of condemnation, so I no longer believed that I could be forgiven. I was convinced that I was condemned until Jesus looked at me and nodded. Jesus did not condemn the woman caught in adultery and Jesus did not condemn me, a woman of the city. Jesus had forgiven me. Like the woman caught in adultery, Jesus had given me a second chance, a new beginning.

I was so filled with gratitude for Jesus' loving forgiveness that I wanted to do something. I wanted him to know how grateful I was for the gift of a fresh start in life that he gave me. I was determined to do something for Jesus who had done so much for me. So, when I heard that Jesus was dining at the home of Simon, the Pharisee, I grabbed the most extravagant gift I had and headed toward the dinner party. With my alabaster flask of ointment in hand, I barged into Simon's house uninvited and unannounced.

I know it was an audacious act on my part; after all, I was an unwelcomed guest at the home of the self-appointed monitor of righteousness. What I did was unimaginable. Women did not intrude into the company of men, especially at dinner. However, I threw out all social niceties and etiquette because I was single minded. I had my mind on thanking Jesus.

As I reached Jesus I was overcome with emotion. Just as Jesus' forgiveness flowed freely, so did my tears. I sobbed at the feet of Jesus thinking of the shackles of guilt and shame I had worn for so long and the gift of freedom that Jesus had given me. The other guests just stared, wide-eyed with their mouths open. I did not care what they thought of me. The tears continued to flow; it was as if my tears were washing away all the pain that I had kept locked in my heart. It felt so good to let go, to know that I did not need to hold onto the bitterness and resentments that I held. The tears were of heartfelt gratitude, and for them I made no apology.

Kneeling at Jesus' feet, I wiped my tears with my hair and lavishly anointed his feet with ointment from the alabaster jar. I poured it out. I poured out all the ointment as a sign of my love and thankfulness. I poured out all that I had.

Simon and the other Pharisees began mumbling against me. They were insinuating that Jesus was wasting his time and energy on me, a sinner. They felt they deserved Jesus' attention and they knew that I certainly did not. Not only did Simon take some jabs at me, he poked a few at Jesus, too.

He said under his breath, but loud enough for everyone to hear, "If this man were a prophet, he would have known who and what sort of woman this is who is touching him, for she is a sinner."

Jesus then said, "Simon, I have something to say to you. A certain creditor had two debtors; one owed 500 denarii, and the other fifty. When they could not pay, he forgave them both. Now which of them will love him more?"

Simon was looking nervous and uncomfortable. Sheepishly he responded, "The one, I suppose, to whom he forgave more."

Jesus had caught Simon flat-footed. "You suppose, Simon? You *suppose?*" Then Jesus turned to me, but spoke to Simon. "Do you see this woman? I entered your house, you gave me no water for my feet, but she was wet my feet with her tears and wiped them with her hair. You gave me no kiss, but from the time I came in she has not ceased to kiss my feet. You did not anoint my head with oil, but she has anointed my feet with ointment. Therefore I tell you, her sins, which are many, are forgiven, for she loved much; but he who is forgiven little, loves little."

Simon seemed surprised. He expected that Jesus would condemn me, but he did not. Instead, Jesus pointed out to Simon two things. First, Simon was remiss in extending the basic courtesies as a host. He did not do what was always done when a guest entered one's home. Simon did not give Jesus the kiss of peace. He did not pour cool water on his feet. He did not place a drop of fragrant ointment on his head. But more importantly, Jesus pointed out to Simon his inability to comprehend the whole matter of forgiveness. Simon just did not get it, because Simon saw no need for forgiveness in his own life. Simon thought of himself as a righteous individual; all was well between him and God. So, he felt he had the right to judge me.

The hate I saw in the eyes of Simon was just the opposite of the look Jesus gave me when Jesus said to me, "Your faith has saved you." I was saved and everything had changed. I was no longer a victim to my own self-loathing. I no longer despised who I was. I no longer hated those who stood in judgment of me. I was loved. I was forgiven. I was transformed into a faithful follower of Jesus.

That is why I poured out all that I had. That is why I poured out the expensive, fragrant ointment. It was the most extravagant gift I had, but I could never give as much as I had been given. The lavish ointment mingled with my tears was only a small token in comparison to the gift Jesus had given me.

Are you like I had been, hungry for a loving forgiveness that brings a fresh start? Or are you like Simon, not seeing your need for the clean slate that forgiveness brings? It does not matter. It does not matter if you are like me or like Simon. Jesus wants to lavishly pour out God's extravagant love on you. Let Jesus anoint you with the gift of his love and forgiveness.

Listen to the words of a very frustrated woman. Martha, the sister of Lazarus and Mary, just wanted to be the perfect hostess. She wanted to prove her worth by having everything under control. Why didn't Jesus understand and tell her lazy sister, Mary, to come and help her? Could it be that Mary understood something she didn't? After Martha walks away from Jesus in a huff, a second encounter with him turns her life around.

A Clarifying Word
Luke 10:38-42

My sister and I are like night and day. We are complete opposites. It seemed to me that she had no motivation. She could sit, reading and praying, all day while ignoring the work that needed to be done. Now I, on the other hand, liked to stay busy. I lived by that old saying, "Busy hands are happy hands." Or, to put it another way, "Idol hands are the work of the devil." I bet some of you have heard that, or maybe you live by that old saying.

When I heard that Jesus and his disciples were coming for dinner, I kicked into high gear. I wanted everything to be perfect. Jesus was not the kind of guest that had high expectations. He wanted to be treated like a family member, but it was my expectations for myself that were high.

There was so much to do. The house needed cleaning, the garden needed weeding, and the food needed preparing. I ran around and around and around, dusting, scrubbing, chopping, kneading, baking, and cooking.

And where was Mary? Where was Mary? That was the question of the day. I did not know where Mary was. The only thing I knew was that she was not helping me. If I were to guess, I would guess that she was off reading or praying while I was frantically preparing for Jesus' arrival.

When it came time to welcome our guests I had everything nearly perfect, but I was exhausted. As you know, there are always many last-minute details to tend to when you are having a large crowd for dinner. The fire needed tending, the pot needed stirring, and the appetizers needed serving. Yet, where was Mary? Where was Mary? She was nowhere to be seen until Jesus and the disciples were at the door. Mary then whisks in to take over as hostess. Looking fresh as a daisy, Mary warmly welcomed Jesus and the disciples and showed them to the living room while I didn't even have an extra minute to welcome the guests. It looked as though she was going to take all the credit for the work I had done.

I could have used Mary's help as I was scurrying about putting the finishing touches on the meal. In my mind, there were 101 things which had to be done, but where was Mary? While I was feverishly working, Mary was sitting at the feet of Jesus drinking in his every word. Mary was giving all her attention to Jesus and not paying attention to the things that needed tending to. She had no idea how much I was doing to prepare the perfect meal. She was not thinking of me, she was only thinking of Jesus. Well, I was seething with anger. I was ready to boil over. I had had enough, so I burst out of the kitchen in tears and said to Jesus, "Jesus, don't you care that I am running around here like mad doing all this work by myself? Tell Mary to help me."

Do you know what Jesus said to me? He said, "Martha, Martha, you are worried and distracted by many things."

The nerve of him, offending me that way! After all, I was trying to be a wonderful hostess and prepare a fantastic meal and he was calling me a worrywart. I just wanted everything to be nice for him. I stomped off into the kitchen and dried my tears with my apron. Then I straightened up and served the meal without the help of Mary. It was a hit. Everyone raved about the food, but their compliments did not make me feel very good about myself.

Before I cleaned up the kitchen, I sat for a long time and stewed like a slow-boiling pot over the fire. I was ashamed of myself, making a fuss like that in front of all my guests. I wondered what on earth had possessed me to behave that way. Then it dawned on me: I had a compulsive need to earn my worth. Work was my identity. My sense of self depended on how that meal turned out, but that was not true for Mary. Mary and I were complete opposites. Mary's worth was grounded by God's love that Jesus talked about.

Jesus' words came back to me, but as my anger subsided I listened to them in a new way. The words rolled over me again and again. "Only one thing is needful, Martha. Mary, your sister, has chosen what is important and that will not be taken away from her."

The tears came again. This time they were not fueled by anger, rather, they were fueled by grief. I grieved what I had missed by being too distracted with my perfectionism. Things became clear to me. I had been so worried about impressing my guests that I had missed the guest, Jesus, all together. I was bound to the superficial things. I was captivated by the external things instead of the one thing that really mattered. I wondered what Mary had learned from Jesus that day that could not be taken from her.

I started to recall things Mary had told me Jesus had said. I never heard his teachings firsthand because I was always too busy. But, it all came rolling back, washing over me like a refreshing mountain stream. "Do not worry about your life, what you will eat or what you will drink, or about your body, what you will wear. Is not life more than food and the body more than clothing? Look at the birds of the air; they neither sow nor reap nor gather into barns, and yet your heavenly Father feeds them. Are you not of more value than they? And can any of you, by worrying, add a single hour to your span of life? But seek first the kingdom of God and God's righteousness, and all these things will be given to you as well."

I heard those words in a whole new way. As I recalled them this time it was clear that I did not need to make things perfect. God's love is perfect and that is sufficient. You know, it doesn't really matter if you get the dusting done. It doesn't matter if you put in an extra ten hours at work. What does it matter if the meals are not perfect or if the clothes are not just right? Those things don't give life. They do not give meaning. They do not give worth. God does. God gives life, that is clear.

Mary had it right. She focused on what gave her life. Mary focused on God, the giver of life. Mary's attention was on her life-line. She knew what fed her spirit. She knew what refreshed and renewed her soul. She knew the source of abundant life.

Mary had it right. I thought I had to be perfect before I could be loved. Mary knew that God loved her despite her imperfections. I thought my self-esteem depended on what I did, but Mary knew that it depended on God's love for her. She had heard Jesus talk again and again of God's love and Mary took that good news to heart.

Mary had it right. She was not frenzied. She did not sweat the little stuff. She was not anxious about the details. Mary was at peace. Her spirit was calmed in the presence of Jesus.

When I would get wound up and move in so many directions that I did not know which way I was going, Mary would often quote her favorite psalm to me, Psalm 46. She would say, "Martha, listen to this, 'Be still and know that I am God.' " Until that day Jesus confronted me about all the unnecessary distractions in my life, I was never still enough to hear those words with my heart. Mary would quote that psalm to me and I would respond, "Yeh, yeh, yeh." But I now wanted the peace that I saw in Mary. I was weary. I was so weary of trying to prove myself.

It suddenly became clear to me that my whole life was driven by fear. It was fear that kept me on the move. It was fear that was the driving force in my life. I feared rejection that I was not good enough. I feared abandonment if I could not make people love me. All my frenzied activity was driven by fear; whereas, Mary's peace was fed with trust.

The tears flowed again: tears of exhaustion, exhaustion from trying to work out my own salvation. I knew I could not do it anymore. I could not keep doing, doing, doing.

Suddenly, someone was touching my shoulder and calling my name. "Martha, I just wanted to thank you for the delicious meal," Jesus then asked, "Martha, are you okay?"

"Oh, Jesus. You were right. Mary has it right. I have missed so much by not sitting at your feet like Mary. I am sorry. I thought that I had to be perfect before you or anyone else would love me. I was so filled with fear I could not stop. That is what you were trying to tell me, wasn't it? You were inviting me to stop running, to not fear and to trust God. Isn't that right, Jesus?" I felt like I could not stop rambling until Jesus said, "Yes, Martha. That is what I want for you."

Jesus went on, "Martha, I want you to hear the words of Isaiah. I want you to take them to heart. 'Now thus says the Lord, he who created you, O Jacob, he who formed you, O Israel; "Fear not, for I have redeemed you; I have called you by name, you are mine.

When you pass through the waters, I will be with you. When you walk through fire you shall not be burned, and the flame shall not consume you. For I am the Lord your God. You are precious in my eyes, and honored, and I love you. Fear not, for I am with you." ' "

Jesus went on, "Martha, I am on my way to Jerusalem. There I will be killed and on the third day rise again, so that you never have to live in fear again. Trust in my love. That is the one thing that is needful. Trust that I love you, Martha."

My tears flowed again, but this time they were tears of loving gratitude. I left the kitchen just as it was and followed Jesus to Jerusalem.

Listen to the words of a desperate woman who has experienced intense pain, both physically and emotionally, for over eighteen years. When she hears a new voice teaching with authority in the temple, little does she realize that she is about to be touched by someone who can heal both her body and her soul. After meeting Jesus, she is no longer a cripple. She stands tall and is, therefore, able to see the needs of others.

A Transforming Word
Luke 13:10-17

Oh, how I suffered. For eighteen years I suffered. I had been sick so long that I forgot what it was like to feel healthy. I lived with constant pain, pain in my back that hounded me morning, noon, and night. It was paralyzing pain. I would wake every morning hoping that the pain would be gone only to find that when I moved, *bang*, the pain was there to destroy my hope of a new day. Day after day, month after month, year after year it was there, the plaguing pain was there.

I am sure that some of you know what it is like to live with chronic pain: the joints that are bone rubbing on bone, the arthritis that hinders movement, the rotator cuff that needs repair, the hip that has worn out. Many of you know the pain that drives one to scream, "Enough is enough. I just can't take it anymore."

But the physical pain was only part of my battle. Being so bent over that I could not see the sky was only a small part of my suffering. What was even more crippling than the physical pain was the emotional torment I endured.

At first, my friends and neighbors were considerate, but then they backed away as if I were contagious. The longer the illness went on, the smaller my world became. I really became a social outcast. No one ever touched me.

Do you know what it feels like to never get a hug, to never see a friendly smile, to never hear the words, "I love you"? I was so lonely. Believe me, my heart ached more than my back did.

Have you ever experienced the crippling effects of emotional pain? Have you ever ached for a loving touch? Has depression stolen your zest for life? Has shame eaten away at your self-esteem? Have you ever felt like you don't fit in? Have you longed to be loved and accepted for who you are? A crippled heart can bring paralyzing pain.

On top of that, on top of the physical and emotional struggles I endured, I felt the heavy weight of spiritual suffering. I had always trusted that God answered prayer, but after eighteen years of praying with no answers, what would you believe? I still went to the temple everyday merely because it was a good place to beg.

My prayers to God had been altered. I was angry. With a bitter edge I cried out with words of the psalmist, "How long O Lord? Wilt thou forget me for ever? How long wilt thou hide thy face from me? How long must I bear this pain in my soul, and have sorrow in my heart all the day?"

The God of steadfast love and enduring mercy no longer felt steadfast to me. In fact, I felt forsaken by God. My spirit ached more than my back. I longed to be in relationship with God, but my bitterness served as a fortress letting neither God nor anyone else close to my heart.

Do you know what I mean? Maybe you have had a hard time making sense of faith when you have watched a loved one suffer or when you have felt the tearing of the heart that grief brings. Maybe you have wondered where God was when you felt lost and lonely. Maybe it has been hard for you to believe in a God who loves you just as you are. We all have those times when our spirit aches for good news, don't we?

Mine was such a time. Everything ached, my body and my spirit. I was at the end of my rope. I was desperate. The physical, emotional, and spiritual suffering was more than I could take.

I did not know what to do. I did not know where to turn. Then one day as I stood begging on the steps of the synagogue, I heard a new voice teaching, a voice of love and yet of authority. For the first time in years, I felt drawn into the synagogue. Of course, I could not stand up straight enough to see who was speaking, but I sensed there was something different about this man. I stood in the background and listened to him speak with loving power.

Suddenly, he stopped. I heard him say, "Come here." I did not move, for I had no idea who he was talking to. The next thing I knew he was kneeling in front of me. I could see him face-to-face.

No one ever bothered to kneel down and look up into my eyes the way he did. His eyes were so loving. He said to me, "Woman, you are set free from your ailment." Then he touched me. No one had touched me in years. He not only touched my arm; he touched my soul. I felt his love, his unconditional love, roll through me like an ocean wave. Then I stood up. I stood up straight! For the first time in eighteen years I could stand up straight. There was no more pain. I could look into the eyes of those around me. It was a miracle. My suffering was over. The pain was gone. I began shouting praises at the top of my lungs.

However, the leader of the synagogue quickly put a stop to that. There was no love there. He did not rejoice with me. No, he looked at me with great disdain and screamed, "Hush, woman!" He then looked at Jesus with white-hot passion. Seething with anger he said to the crowd in an accusatory manner, "There are six days on which work ought to be done; come on those days and be cured, and not on the sabbath day."

The nerve of him! I was ready to speak up in defense of Jesus when Jesus spoke to the temple leaders, "You hypocrites! Does not each of you on the sabbath untie his ox or his donkey from the manger and lead it away to give it water? And ought not this woman, a daughter of Abraham whom Satan bound for eighteen years, be set free from this bondage on the sabbath day?"

Well, that put them to shame. They bit their tongues and I stood speechless as well. For the first time someone understood my suffering. Jesus understood that I was in bondage to my suffering. I was trapped with no way out. Jesus knew that my pain had paralyzed me physically, emotionally, and spiritually.

Through his loving touch I felt like I belonged. I can hardly find the words to describe how I felt when Jesus called me a daughter of Abraham and Sarah. I had been alienated from the community, especially the community of faith, and Jesus invited me back in. I belonged. I was accepted. I was loved.

His loving understanding transformed me. My self-esteem soared. The monkey of self-loathing was lifted from my back and I stood up. I stood tall. I was more important than the law. Jesus was telling me his love for me, and for all people, was more important than all the rules and regulations the synagogue leaders insisted on. Jesus loved me more than the law! In his eyes, my well-being came first. Wow! No one had ever treated me with such love, dignity, or respect. Jesus touched me with his love and I was transformed. I was a new person. The whole world looked different to me. I looked at everything and everyone through the same lens that Jesus did, through the lens of unconditional love. My envy and jealousy of those around me dissolved. My hatred of those who mocked me or ignored no longer consumed me. The compassion and empathy I felt toward those who were driven by self-righteous judgment surprised me.

The anger I felt toward God changed to love. The walls I created, to keep myself from God, tumbled down. I knew that the promises in God's Word were true. Indeed, I once again believed that God is merciful, slow to anger, and abounding in steadfast love. My prayers of lament turned to the poetry of praise.

Those who saw the power of Jesus' transforming love rejoiced with me. They joined in my joyful song and dance. With one voice we sang out the psalmist's words:

> *Praise the Lord! Praise God in his sanctuary; praise him in his mighty firmament! Praise him for his mighty deeds; praise him according to his exceeding greatness! Praise him with trumpet sound; praise him with lute and harp! Praise him with timbrel and dance; praise him with strings and pipe!*
> — Psalm 150:1-6

I praised God for God's transforming power in my life. Before Jesus touched me, the only thing I could see was my own pain, but the power of Jesus' love changed all that. My eyes were open to the suffering of others. I felt called to serve those who suffered from physical pain. I felt called to serve those who were in emotional anguish; those who felt alienated, those who felt no hope, those who felt unloved, and those who felt unworthy. I felt called to serve those who were spiritually paralyzed; those who had lost their faith;

who could no longer trust in God's steadfast love or who were consumed with bitterness. The whole focus of my life changed from focusing on me to focusing on serving others. What a miraculous transformation!

Jesus' loving touch is amazing! It has the power to heal our aching bodies, emotions, and spirits. It has the ability to transform our vision. Our lives and the world look different through the lens of God's transforming love. Jesus' love has the capacity to call us from being self-serving people to being God-serving neighbors who see beyond our own pain with an empathetic eye and compassionate touch toward others' physical, emotional, or spiritual discomforts.

Jesus touched me and my life was fully transformed and I then stood tall, ready to serve.

Whatever it is that cripples you this day, whether you are bent over from chronic pain, by the burdens of stress, from the heaviness of guilt, or by the challenges of doubt, let Jesus' love transform you and then stand tall to serve the God of transforming love.

Listen to the words of a woman who was forced to live her life in exile because of the dreaded disease of leprosy. As you listen, try to imagine how you would feel if you were to contract a disease that would take you away from life as you know it. Enter Jesus! One brief encounter with him should have changed this woman's life dramatically. Why didn't it change her spirit as well as her body?

A Grateful Word
Luke 17:11-19

You cannot imagine what life was like for us lepers. It was desperately depressing. We had no hope, absolutely no hope. Leprosy was a horrendous disease that took a physical, emotional, and spiritual toll.

We had terrible sores all over our bodies, uncomfortable, ugly, ugly sores. As my disease progressed, my lips, nose, and ear lobes grew thicker and thicker until my face looked like that of a wild beast. Then my limbs became horribly mutilated and in time I began loosing my fingers and toes. It was a slow death with no hope for a cure.

But the physical pain was not the worst part of being a leper. The emotional pain was devastating. My life as I knew it ended when I got leprosy. My hopes and dreams for the future were dashed. Jewish law required me to leave my family. What kind of law would make a mother leave her children? How could that be what God wanted for me and my family?

Death would have been far easier than exile. You should have seen my children's faces when I told them I had to go away. They didn't understand. How could they? They were so young. They wanted their mother. They needed me. They did not care if I was sick. They did not care what I looked like. They just wanted me to be with them.

I thought my heart would break the day that I left my family. I knew my husband would take good care of the children, but I wanted to be there for them. I wanted to watch them grow up. I wanted to hold them when they were hurt and comfort them when they were afraid. I wanted to laugh with them and cry with them. Leprosy took that away from me. It took my role as a mother away. The emotional pain of my many losses: my health, my family, my home, was beyond words.

Leprosy also robbed me of my faith. I wondered what kind of God would allow this to happen to me. No one could do anything bad enough to deserve such a terrible, terrible disease. But I knew that is what people thought of me. After all, that is what they were taught in the synagogue. The religious leaders convinced people that those with leprosy deserved the awful disease. It was a punishment for a sin. Lepers were viewed as unclean. My faith community abandoned me in my time of need. There was no love there, only rejection and judgment. It was hard to believe in a loving God when you did not feel the love of God's people. So, I wondered what the point was of worshiping with those who despised me? What was the point of praising God when leprosy stripped me of everything I held dear: my health, my family, my community, and my faith?

I had become a despairing outcast. Like wild animals, lepers lived in open pits, caves, or anywhere else we could find shelter outside the city limits. No healthy person was allowed to come within fifty yards of us. That was the Jewish law. Whenever someone began to approach, we were to cry out, "Unclean, unclean." How do you think that would make you feel? Let me tell you, I felt like dirt. That was all that I had to cover my shame — dirt and filth. I spent my days begging for food and my nights praying for death. There was little to console me, but one thing helped. A small consolation was that I was not the only one. Misery loves company. There were ten of us that lived together. Misery is a great equalizer. It did not matter if you were rich or poor, wife or widower, Gentile or Jew. We were all unclean lepers.

We even had a Samaritan living with us. I never would have associated with a Samaritan when I was healthy. The priests had always told us that they were like dogs, half-breeds who were dirty scum. That no longer mattered among us lepers. The presence of a Samaritan couldn't make us anymore unclean than we already were.

Ten pathetic lepers created our community. Despite our care for one another, life was miserable. We were consumed by hopelessness. Day after day we waited for our only hope of release:

death. Have you ever been that desperate? Have things ever become that bleak? Have clouds of darkness consumed you?

We were without hope until one day we heard that Jesus was coming. We were filled with a glimmer of hope as we wondered if he would heal us. We had heard that he had the power to heal lepers. So, as we saw a crowd approaching on the road, we cried at the top of our lungs, "Jesus, Master, have mercy on us."

Then an amazing thing happened. Jesus stopped. Most people moved as far away as possible and pretended that we did not exist but, Jesus stopped. He stopped, looked each of us in the eye and said, "Go and show yourselves to the priests."

We wasted no time. We knew what those words meant. Jesus was telling us we would be healed. You see there were elaborate rules for the cleansing of lepers. One of those rules was the priest had to declare a leper clean before he or she returned to a normal life.

When Jesus said, "Go and show yourselves to the priests," we trusted he would heal us. We ran as fast as our marred limbs would carry us hoping we would be given the okay to return to a full life again.

As I made my way to the synagogue I began to notice a dramatic change. There was a cool sensation on my parched skin. Then I suddenly noticed that my hands were free of sores and my legs were no longer disfigured and discolored.

Feeling a newfound health, the others and I began to run faster and faster. We wanted to have our healing confirmed by the priest. We hurried to do just what Jesus had told us, so we did not think to turn around and thank him. We were merely doing as we were told. Jesus had said we should go to the priest and, as law-abiding citizens, that is what we did.

There was one of the ten that stopped — the Samaritan. We yelled for him to hurry up but he said he needed to find Jesus to thank him. We figured there would always be time to give thanks. There was no stopping us! We wanted to get to the priest as soon as possible. The sooner we saw the priest, the sooner we could get back to life as we knew it.

Once I had been to the priest, I was too anxious to see my children, so I had no time to turn around and thank Jesus. I wanted to catch up on all that I had missed. I wanted to hold them in my arms and smother them with kisses. Thinking about giving Jesus thanks was the last thing on my mind. My thoughts were on seeing my family.

The reunion was wonderful. Oh, you cannot imagine our joy. Being together was fabulous. Very quickly, we got back into a normal routine, and I got so busy with family life that I forgot to thank Jesus.

That was the difference between the Samaritan and the rest of us who were healed that day. He remembered to give thanks and because of that his healing was complete. He was healed physically and spiritually. The miserable disease of leprosy had been lifted from all of us, but the misery of ingratitude continued to weigh heavy on those of us who did not give thanks. Our bodies were healed, but our spirits were not. Only the Samaritan experienced full healing. He lived beyond obedience into joyful gratitude. His spirit was full of life, life that comes through praise, worship, and gratitude to God.

My body was healthy, but I was not healed. Although I was back with my family, I regret the day that I ran off to the priest to have my healing verified. I regret not stopping to give thanks to Jesus. My heart remained marred. I was not full of life and joy like the Samaritan. I hope and pray that you do not make the same mistake that I did. I beg you to stop this day and every day to give thanks to God.

I had good excuses. I wanted to follow Jesus' instructions. I wanted to see my children. After all, I was their mother and they needed me. I got too busy doing all the things that I was supposed to do. All of my excuses were good ones, so I thought I was justified in not giving thanks to Jesus.

The other lepers had equally good excuses, too. One of them was a priest before he got leprosy. He was in a hurry to get back to doing God's work. Another leper had gotten leprosy by caring for his sick wife. She had died of leprosy and he was too consumed with grief to give thanks. One of the lepers was a little girl. She had lived with lepers most of her life, so the other lepers never taught her to be thankful. There was one among us who had lived with leprosy so long that he was not sure he wanted to start over. He was too confused to give thanks. Oh, yes, all but the Samaritan had their excuses for not turning back to give thanks to Jesus.

I am sure that you have a few excuses of your own for not giving thanks to God. Maybe you are too busy climbing the corporate ladder or playing taxi for the children. Possibly you feel you don't have much to be thankful for.

Maybe you have doubts about God's steadfast love because your prayers have not been answered the way that you want.

The excuses are always there, but I beg you to stop and give thanks. I don't want your heart to be heavy like mine. An ungrateful heart eats away at the joy of life. An ungrateful heart blinds us to all the blessings God has given us. It turns us inward.

The religious outcast had it right. The Samaritan showed us just how holy his heart was as he was filled with exuberant praise and extravagant gratitude. Be one in ten. Stop and give thanks this day!

Listen to the words of a woman who could not forgive herself for the sins in her past. Five divorces, and now she was living with someone who did not love her enough to marry her. No wonder she made her way to the village well when she was sure no one else was there. But on this day she encounters Jesus, who offers her more than water. She receives living *water that quenches more than physical thirst.*

A Refreshing Word
John 4:1-30

It was a hot, dry day. The wind howled and the dust blew. About noon, I went to the well just like I did everyday. Everyday I needed to get water; water to wash with, water to cook with, and water to drink. Water. It is essential for life. Without it, one cannot live. I despised going to the well, but it had to be done.

The well in our little town was the gathering place. It was the place where all the women met to pick up the local gossip, which is exactly why I did not go to the well. I *was* the local gossip. I went to the well when the noon sun baked the ground and people alike. I went in the heat of the day to avoid the women rolling their eyes and turning their backs when they saw me coming. It was easier to face the heat than to experience their looks of red-hot condemning judgment.

One day when I was at the well, I saw a stranger resting there. I could not figure it out, because men did not gather at the well. That was women's work. What was even more surprising was that he was a Hebrew. The Hebrews despised Samaritans so much that they rarely walked through Samaria. In fact, they usually walked around Samaria even though it added miles to their trip. Normally they went to great extremes to avoid any contact with Samaritans.

I tried to ignore him by busying myself at the well. I was so startled when he spoke to me that I dropped my bucket. You see, men were not supposed to speak to women in public, so when he asked me for a drink I stood in stunned disbelief. He repeated himself, "Give me a drink."

He was bold, asking me, a Samaritan woman, for a drink. I asked him, "How is it that you, a Jew, ask a drink from me, a woman of Samaria? For Jews have no dealings with Samaritans."

He gave me a strange answer saying, "If you knew the gift of God, and who it is that is saying to you, 'Give me a drink,' you would have asked him, and he would have given you living water." I had no idea what he was talking about. Living water? I poked a little fun at him. Here he was talking about giving me living water, yet I was the one with the rope and bucket. I said, "This well is deep. How do you expect to get this living water? Do you think you are better than Jacob who started this well?"

The answer that I received was even stranger. It seemed like we were having two separate conversations. He replied, "Everyone who drinks of this water will thirst again, but whoever drinks of the water that I shall give will never thirst; the water that I shall give will become a spring of water welling up to eternal life." That sounded great to me. I lived in a dry, arid land. The sun parched everything, land and body alike. I would welcome a spring of water that would free me of the burdensome task of going to the well everyday. So, I said, "Sir, give me this water, that I may not thirst, nor come here to draw."

He then changed the whole direction of the conversation. Out of the blue he said to me, "Go, call your husband, and come here." I was bewildered. What is with this guy? One minute we were talking about water and the next minute he was asking me to get my husband. Normally, I would try to cover my shame by lying, but there was something about this stranger that invited me to speak the truth. I said, "I have no husband."

I was stunned by his reply. He said, "What you say is true. You do not have a husband. You have had five husbands and the man that you are living with now is not your husband."

Oh, the truth can hurt. He spoke the truth. That is exactly why I came to the well in the afternoon. I was shunned by all because I had been married so many times. After five divorces no man wanted me, so I was living with a man I was not married to. Indeed, he spoke the truth. I figured what was coming next was some kind of lecture about what a rotten person I was. I had heard it all before from people who judged me with their self-righteous attitudes. I braced myself for what was coming next, harsh condemnation. I did not need him to write me off as a lost cause, because I had written myself off. I hated myself. I was my own worst critic. I took to heart all the condemning judgments spoken against me through the years. No one had to tell me that I was a bad person. Shame was my cloak. Self-loathing was my constant companion. Listening to him condemn me was the last thing I needed, so I changed the subject. I thought he was a rabbi, so to get the focus off of me, I changed the subject to religion. I thought if I got him talking about religion that he would stop probing into my mistakes and failures. I tried to get him caught up with some meaningless discussion on religion.

But he did not play along. I asked him about the proper place for worship, but basically he turned that question around to me again. What he said to me was that where you worship is not the important thing. Rather, what is important is the spirit in which you worship. The way that I understood that was that one needs to bring the truth of one's personal integrity to worship. Worship means coming before God with a spirit of reverence and love.

As our conversation continued, I told him that I knew the Messiah, God's chosen one, was coming. Then he said the most remarkable thing. He said, "I who speak to you am he."

I believed him immediately. I sensed there was something different about him. He did not shun me. He knew my story without me even telling him and he did not turn his back. He did not write me off as a lost cause like I had written myself off.

Sometimes, we are our own worst enemies, aren't we? Have you ever done something wrong and been unable to forgive yourself? Or worse yet, have you internalized your mistakes and believed that you are a bad person because of it? Have you been convinced that you could never be forgiven? Have you ever felt like you were a lost cause?

That is how I felt, but that is not how Jesus felt about me. He made me take a second look at myself, because he did not treat me like I was a lost cause. No, he treated me with loving acceptance. In his presence, I felt like a whole new person. Everyone else had written me off. I was a social outcast.

But he was different. It was refreshing. He accepted me for who I was. He was full of love. He had a forgiving heart.

51

Suddenly, I realized how thirsty I was and it was not a physical thirst. It was a spiritual thirst. I was thirsty for love, acceptance, and forgiveness. I was tired of being empty and lonely, of feeling unloved and unaccepted, of experiencing the heavy burden of shame and guilt. I was weary from having my self-esteem defined by others. I wanted something deeper. I wanted more to life than mere existence. I was thirsty to know God in spirit and truth. I longed to drink from the deep well of God's grace.

Have you felt like you were living in a spiritual desert? That is where I had been living for years. It was as if Jesus held up a mirror and I could see how dehydrated I was. When I found Jesus, the Messiah, I realized that I had been going from well to well but seeking life in all the wrong places. It was Jesus that led me to the well that refreshed my parched spirit.

It was Jesus, the Messiah, that brought me to the life-giving water of God's love. I could hardly wait to share the spring of living water welling up inside of me. I had come to the well to draw water and I was given so much more. Living water, I was given an eternal stream of living water! At the well, I found my Savior, the Messiah. I was so excited that I ran back to the village to tell the people what I had experienced. I stirred up the entire town. I, the woman the townspeople shunned, got everyone to listen to me. They saw the new life in me. They saw the cloak of shame had been lifted. They saw the joy. They saw the peace. They saw the hope. They knew something was different and they wanted to know what had happened.

I wanted to scream from the mountaintop that no one can limit the scope of God's love. I wanted to let everyone know that if the living water is available to me it is available to anyone. No person, no race, no gender, no sinner is exempt from God's grace.

I went and told them the truth. I told everyone in the village that Jesus had told me everything I had ever done. That made the people curious enough to go and see Jesus for themselves. I wanted everybody to have the same opportunity as I had. I wanted everyone to taste the living water themselves. I wanted them to meet the Messiah and live.

You know I want the same for you, too. What are you thirsty for? Are you thirsting for self-esteem? Let Jesus quench your thirst with his unconditional love. Has an unforgiven sin parched your soul? Then come and be washed in the living water of God's forgiveness. Do you long for a drink of acceptance? The fountain of God's loving acceptance can replenish you. Come to the well. Come taste the living water. Come and drink in the gifts of God's love, acceptance, and forgiveness. It will refresh you and you will never be thirsty again.

Listen to the words of a woman who felt God had forgotten her in her hour of deepest need. Mary, the sister of Lazarus and Martha, was sure that Jesus would come and heal her brother. But he did not come, and Lazarus died! Why did he wait to come? Why did he not work according to her timetable? Mary encounters a grieving Messiah and learns that Jesus feels loss just as deeply as she does. The end of her story is worth the wait.

The Living Word
John 11:1-45

We took good care of my brother when he got sick. My sister and I did absolutely everything we could do. We tended to his every need, but it didn't seem to help. Lazarus got sicker and sicker as each moment passed. We called the doctor, but he had no idea what was wrong. When I looked in the doctor's eyes, I knew that Lazarus was gravely ill. I knew that he was teetering on the fine line between life and death. I felt helpless and afraid. I could not think straight. Finally, my sister suggested we send for Jesus. He was one of Lazarus' good friends and he was the only one who could do something. He was our only hope. We had seen him perform many miracles. We were there when he turned water into wine. The disciples had told us how Jesus had calmed the storm on the Sea of Galilee. He had even given sight to the blind man who used to beg on the steps of the synagogue. If anyone could make Lazarus well it would be Jesus. So, we sent a message that Lazarus was deathly ill.

We had no doubt that Jesus would heal Lazarus.

We waited and waited and waited. The minutes turned to hours. The hours turned to days and Jesus did not come. We waited and Lazarus became sicker. His breathing became slower and slower. He labored for every breath. We waited. While praying to God, we waited. Lazarus lost consciousness. We waited. While holding his hand, we waited. We could not understand what was taking Jesus so long. We waited. While pleading to God, we waited. We waited until it was too late. Jesus did not come and Lazarus died.

We watched him take his last breath. It was devastating. It felt like a part of me died. My emotions rushed through me like a raging river: the sadness, the loneliness, the confusion, the disbelief, the anger. I could not believe that I would never see my brother

57

again. I longed to see his smile, to hear his laugh, and to feel his strong hand on my shoulder.

I wondered why, why did my brother have to die? Why now, when he was so young and had so much life ahead of him? Why didn't Jesus come to help his good friend? Then, Jesus finally came, but he was too late, and I was angry. My first inclination was to ignore Jesus, but when I saw the pain in his eyes I knew that he was hurting as well. Grief calls out to grief, so I ran to meet him. I knew he understood the depth of my pain because he loved Lazarus, too.

I felt confused. Although it was comforting to see Jesus, I still felt angry. I did not exactly greet him warmly. In the pain of my grief, I chided him saying, "It is too late. He's dead. Your friend is dead. If only you would have been here earlier my brother would still be alive." If only, if only, if only ... that was my mantra of grief. If only something could have been done so that I could have my brother back. If only I would not have to be feeling this pain. If only Jesus would have come when we called for him.

The unanswerable questions played over and over again. Why? Why my brother? Where was God? The questions raged within me like a river flooding its banks.

But, the raging waters subsided when I saw Jesus' tears flowing. Jesus wept and I knew that he cared. Jesus cared enough to cry with us. There was comfort in people being willing to share our pain. That is what Jesus did for Martha and me.

He shared our pain. He wept with us. It may not seem like a lot, but it was comforting to have someone weep with us. There were no words Jesus could share to take away our pain, but his tears were enough. His tears said it all. We knew Jesus was there to walk with us in our grief.

Jesus asked to go with us to the grave. As we stood at the graveside, it felt like the reality of grief was beginning to sink deeper. Lazarus was dead. There was no denying that. As I stared at the tomb, dazed by the reality of death, I barely heard Jesus say, "Roll the stone away." I could not believe my ears. I thought Jesus had lost his mind. Lazarus had been dead for four days! I wondered if

Jesus was so distraught that he was unable to think clearly. I said, "Did you say roll away the stone?"

"Yes, roll it away," Jesus said.

I responded, "You have got to be kidding, Jesus. He is dead and he has been dead for four days. The smell will be more than I can bear."

With great compassion Jesus reminded me of what he had said earlier. "Mary," Jesus said, "I am the resurrection and the life, anyone who believes in me, though he dies, will live, and whoever lives and believes in me shall never die."

Then he said, "If you believe you will see the glory of God."

I believed and I saw it. I saw the glory of God. I experienced the glory of God!

We rolled the stone away and the stench was unbearable. Everyone stepped back except Jesus. He moved forward, said a prayer of thanks, and with a loud voice he cried, "Lazarus, come out."

My brother walked out of the tomb. Can you imagine? Lazarus walked out of the tomb and stood before us still bound in his stinking grave clothes. He stood right in front of us. Then Jesus simply said, "Unbind him and let him go free."

Talk about the glory of God. My brother who had been dead for four days was alive. Lazarus was alive.

Jesus had turned our despair into hope. He turned our sorrow into joy. Jesus turned our turmoil into peace. Jesus turned death into life. Jesus did not just bring Lazarus to life; he brought the whole community to life. The whole community came alive with the glory of God. By raising my brother from the dead, Jesus taught everyone that with God all things are possible. Jesus showed us that God is a God who can not only breathe new life into dry bones, but can also breathe new life into dry and broken spirits. Jesus revealed to us that with God there is always hope.

It is easy to lose heart and hope. Maybe for you, it was when one disappointment after another hit you. For others, it could have been when you received a bad diagnosis. Maybe for some, it was when your schedule got out of hand and the pressures of balancing everything became overwhelming. Yet, for others, it may have been the breach of trust and betrayal of loved ones. Others may have lost heart and hope when the nations of the world seem to be constantly at war.

But, with God, there is hope because we have a God who is with us in the distressing times of life. That is what I learned when Jesus wept with us. We have a God who knows our pain firsthand, when life's journey takes us through the dark valley of shadows and sorrows. We have a God who knows the depth and breadth of human emotion. Each of us faces suffering at some time or another and when it comes, one thing we can count on is that God is hurting with us and that God will love us through it. God will walk through the valley with us.

Jesus did that for Martha and me and Jesus will do that for you, too. That is the promise that Jesus gave after his resurrection when he said, "Lo, I am with you always until the close of the age."

Not only do you and I have a God who goes with us, we also have a God who is a resurrecting God. The day that Jesus said, "Lazarus, come out," was the day I knew that our hope in God is not reserved for another day, another life, another world. When Jesus raised my brother, he showed people that God's resurrecting power is available to everyone — now. The promise of an abundant, resurrected life is not reserved for a pie-in-the-sky moment. It is for the present moment.

Today, Jesus calls you forth. Jesus calls you out of the tomb of sin and into a life of forgiveness. You need not be bound by the past. You do not need to be fettered to mistakes you have made, nor to regrets that you hold. You do not need to be tied to the hurts and heartaches of yesterday. Today, Jesus says, "Unbind him. Unbind her."

Come out of the tomb of turmoil and breathe in the freshness of God's peace. You do not need to be bound by worries and anxieties. Jesus calls you to be free as he says, "Come to me all who are heavy laden and I will give you rest."

You are called out of the tomb of doubt and filled with the life of faith. Jesus unlocks the chains of self-doubt and invites you to trust in God. Jesus invites you to trust that you are a loved child of God.

Today, Jesus calls you out of the lonely tomb and into the gift of his companionship. Step out of the tomb and be surrounded by the community of God's people. Step out of the tomb and bask in the sunshine of God's love.

The resurrection of Lazarus gave my sister and me a glimpse of Jesus as Lord and liberator. Jesus brings resurrection to all who long for life in the dry valley. Jesus gives life where there is no life, hope where there is no hope, laughter where there is only sorrow, and peace where there are only storms.

In the resurrection of my brother, we got a glimpse of the abundant life Jesus can give, but it was in the resurrection of Jesus himself that we saw most clearly the power of God's love to give life right now. The resurrection is not something that we need to wait for until we die. Today, Jesus calls you to come out of the tomb of whatever it is that binds you. Come out of the tomb of whatever keeps you from living an abundant, resurrected life. Shake off the grave clothes, like Lazarus did, and live in the grace of God's love.

Listen to the words of a mother who had lost all hope for her daughter's healing. She had already taken her to every doctor she could find. No one could help. They were saying that her daughter was possessed by a demon. No wonder she persistently begs Jesus to heal her daughter. When she encounters Jesus, not only does he heal her daughter, he gives her back the one thing she had lost and needed most — hope.

A Hopeful Word
Mark 7:24-37

Let me tell you about my daughter. Of course, just like any mother, I am biased. But, just the same, she was beautiful. She was born with dark hair and lots of it. It was a stunning contrast to her olive-colored skin. And smiles! Oh, you would never find a child who could brighten up a room with her smile more than my child.

She was the apple of my eye. I just delighted in watching her explore her world. I adored her. I adored everything about her. So, you can just imagine what it was like for me when she got sick. I did not know what was wrong. It was terrible, really terrible, when suddenly my little darling started having these spells. She was not the little girl I knew and loved. She would become unpredictably wild, throwing herself about, unable to speak intelligently, screaming at the top of her lungs. Then, as quickly as the spell came on, it would be gone and she would lie still, staring blankly into space for hours. After that she would once again become the daughter I knew and loved until it started all over again. It was horrible.

I brought her to every kind of doctor I could find, but they could tell me nothing. They did not know what caused these attacks and they did not know how to stop them. My hopes would soar anytime someone would tell me of a new doctor in the area. But my hopes would be quickly dashed when I heard again, "I cannot do anything for her."

Can you imagine my pain as I watched her suffer? If only I could have done something to help her. I felt so frustrated. I felt so helpless. I wanted some answers. Finally, the doctors said, "It must be a demon. Your daughter is possessed by a demon." Well, that was not the answer I was looking for! I did not want to believe them. How could my sweet, beautiful little girl be possessed by a demon?

65

I felt tormented by the label people were putting on her. But, you know, when she was having one of those spells, I have to admit that I was afraid of her. She was wild and she possessed an uncontrollable strength. Her strength was greater than that of a grown man. There was no one that could hold her down. Even I, her own mother, was afraid of her.

At first, the spells came only once in a while, but as time went on they were more and more frequent. She was having them several times a day. I was worried that she was going to hurt herself or hurt someone else. Surely, she was not in her right mind.

I was not a religious woman by any stretch of the word. In fact, my people were enemies of the Hebrews. We did not like them and we did not like their god much better. But, it was in sheer desperation that I began to pray to God for help. There was nothing else I could do. There was nowhere else to turn.

That is when I heard about Jesus, the Hebrew carpenter, who was going about the region of Galilee preaching, teaching, and healing the sick. Now Galilee was a long way from my hometown and I knew there was no way that I could travel that far with my daughter. What if she had a fit along the way? I did not feel comfortable bringing her out of the house. I was afraid the authorities would see her and take her away from me. I was afraid that they would see that I could not control her and deem me as an unfit mother.

Traveling across a whole country to find Jesus was out of the question. However, I dreamed that he would be the answer. I heard rumors that he was making the dumb speak, the blind see, the lame walk, and the deaf hear, so I was confident that he would be able to help my daughter. Although I had hope in his ability, I had no hope that I would be able to get my daughter to him.

One day, I heard he was in the town down the road. I could not imagine that the rumor was true. After all, Jesus rarely stepped foot in our region. The Hebrews considered us to be unclean heathens, so they preferred to walk miles out of their way instead of walking through our countryside.

If Jesus was near, I had to find him. I just had to find him. I searched and searched. It was difficult to find him, because every time I inquired about his whereabouts, the Hebrews just turned their backs on me. They would not give me the time of day because I was a Gentile.

Once I found him I put my pride aside and begged him to help me. Falling at his feet, I begged. I groveled. With great persistence I pleaded for his help.

His response was shocking. I had heard that he was a loving man, but he showed me no love. His response was curt and cutting. Do you know what he called me? He called me a dog. A dog! I would not even say that to my worst enemy. But, that is what he called me. What had I done to deserve that kind of treatment? No one deserves to be called a dog. He said to me, "Let the children first be fed, for it is not right to take the children's bread and throw it to the dogs."

What would you do if someone called you a dog? I think you would probably do what most people would, either hall off and deck him or huff away in anger.

But you must remember I was desperate, absolutely desperate, to help my daughter. And I knew, deep down, that he could help her. So, I swallowed my pride and continued with my persistent plea saying, "Yes, Lord: yet even dogs under the table eat the children's crumbs."

I merely wanted him to know that as an outsider to the faith even the crumbs would do. I was not demanding much from him. I had no claims on him, but I sincerely believed that just a little of his help would be enough. I was persistent in my belief that he could help me. I refused to be ignored. I refused to be put off. I believed that he was my only hope.

And he was! He was my only hope. He made my daughter well. He said, "You may go your way; the demon has left your daughter." He merely spoke the words and she was well. I went home and found that my beautiful child was once again herself. The demon was gone. There were no more spells. No more attacks. Jesus made her well! Life was filled with hope again.

Have you felt hopeless? It is a terrible spot to be in. It is hard to get oneself up in the morning and face another day, isn't it?

Have you ever felt desperate? Have you watched a loved one suffer or have you suffered yourself in a desperate situation: from addiction, with cancer, from a broken heart, with Alzheimer's, from depression?

Maybe most of you don't know what it is like to actually have a demon, but I know you have experienced the feeling of being trapped. Some feel trapped in the guilt of unforgiven sin. Others feel trapped by a cloak of shame and self-loathing. Some may experience the trap of the vicious cycle of domestic violence. Yet others know the trap of a life void of meaning and purpose. Everyone has experienced the sense of entrapment at one time or another, right? We have all run into situations where we did not know what to do or where to turn. The circumstances in life can often make us feel out of control and trapped, can't they?

Those are the times for persistence. Those are the times for persistent faith in the God of hope. Don't give up. Keep going to God. Keep on praying. Keep on hoping. Persistently believe that difficult times, struggles with illness, hopeless days, or nagging fear do not have the last word.

God does have the last word, and it is a word of victory. Just as sickness did not have the last word for my daughter, life's hardships will not have the last word for you. Listen to these words of Isaiah 35:3-4, words of promised hope: "Strengthen the weak hands, and make firm the feeble knees. Say to those who have a fearful heart, 'be strong, fear not' ... for behold your God will come to save you. Then when God comes again, the eyes of the blind shall be opened, and the ears of the deaf unstopped, then shall the lame leap like a deer and the tongue of the dumb sing for joy."

Physically, my daughter was healed and I sang for joy! But she was not the only one who experienced the healing power of God. I experienced it, too. I began to believe in the God of hope. I came to believe that God would stand with me in all things. I believed that God's presence would be with me in all things. That is what gave me hope. Before I met Jesus, I felt all alone in the world. But once I met Jesus, I knew that I was not alone. God stood with me and God stands with you. That is God's promise.

Listen; just listen to God's promise for you:

But, now thus says the Lord who created you, O Jacob, he who formed you, O Israel: "Fear not, for I have redeemed you; I have called you by name, you are mine. When you pass through the waters I will be with you; and through the rivers, they shall not overwhelm you; when you walk through fire you shall not be burned, and the flame shall not consume you. For I am the Lord your God, the Holy One of Israel, your Savior. I give Egypt as your ransom, Ethiopia and Seba in exchange for you.... Fear not, for I am with you; I will bring your offspring from the east, and from the west I will gather you ..." — Isaiah 43:1-3, 5

You know, life was not perfect for us after we were touched by Jesus' healing love. There were new challenges and struggles. There were different hardships and heartaches, but there was hope. We lived in the hope of God's presence and there is no better place to be.

Be persistent in your faith. Have hope. God is with you.

69

Listen to the words of a confused mother who struggles to determine why the same crowd that cheered her son one day was calling for his death in less than a week. Mary gives us a view of the holy week that is seldom considered — the view of the mother of Jesus. She tries unsuccessfully to understand why her son has to suffer so much until she encounters the risen Lord. Then it all makes sense.

A Victorious Word
Mark 11:1-11

The city was packed with Passover pilgrims filled with hopeful expectation. People were abuzz about my son, Jesus. The talk on the street was the speculation about Jesus being the anointed One that God's chosen people had been waiting for. For a people who longed for a leader, like King David, who could free them from Roman occupation and restore Israel's power as a nation, the talk of Jesus being such a leader filled everyone with hope.

People lined the streets in parade-like fashion with enthusiastic anticipation when they heard Jesus was coming. It was exciting. The young and the old waved palm branches and cheered, shouting, "Hosanna! Blessed is he who comes in the name of the Lord. Hosanna in the highest heaven." As Jesus passed by, they laid their coats before him.

As I look back on it now, I wonder if the contrast between Jesus' humble entry into the city and the people's expectation of a powerful king is what radically changed the people's hearts and minds. One day they were shouting, "Hosanna" and a few days later they were screaming, "Crucify him." The messages were mixed. You see, Jesus was not riding some military stallion worthy a king; rather he was riding a donkey fit for a lonely servant.

The people wanted a king with military might, not a humble servant like my son. They sought someone who would squash their enemies underfoot, not a leader who would bow low enough to wash the feet of others. So, the parade-like atmosphere and joyful welcome Jesus received was unsettling for me.

I knew that my son was not the kind of person who would seek power through military strength. He believed in the power of God's love which was opposite of what people were hoping for in the Messiah. I knew my son had a way of agitating people, especially

73

those in authority. I did not think that Jesus' warm reception would sit well with the religious leaders. In fact, I had warned Jesus many times that he was creating enemies by calling the Pharisees a brood of vipers, by challenging the rich, and by spending time with the outcasts of society.

I had heard rumors that the rulers of the day were out to get him. Jesus seemed to threaten the religious leaders. His welcome into Jerusalem added fuel to their fire. They seethed with jealousy as Jesus captured the attention of the entire city. I realize now that it was the groundswell of support that Jesus got as people lined the streets of Jerusalem that spurred the jealous religious leaders to begin in earnest to carry out their plans to kill Jesus.

Indeed, I had an unsettled feeling about Jesus' entry into Jerusalem, because I knew that Jesus expected trouble. As his mom, I could see it in his eyes. For a young man, he talked a lot about his own death saying things like, "The Son of Man came not to be served but to serve, and to give his life as a ransom for many," or "The Son of Man will be betrayed into human hands and they will kill him, and on the third day he will be raised." It was terrible to hear my son talk that way. But there was no stopping him. I had tried. He was determined. He was on God's path.

Oh, I wish I could have protected my boy from all that was going to take place in the days following that Palm Sunday parade. Those of you who are parents know that it is a parent's instinct to want to protect our children from harm, no matter what their age. My heart ached as the week unfolded.

First, it was the feast of Passover where Jesus spoke of the betrayal of one his disciples. For the Passover meal, Jesus gathered with his closest friends. I remember the embarrassment that Peter felt when Jesus began washing his feet. He did not think that Jesus should stoop so low. But, that was my boy. He always saw himself as a loving servant and he was teaching the disciples that they, too, would be called to a live a life of loving service to the world.

He said to them, "Do you know what I have done to you? You call me Teacher and Lord; and you are right, for so I am. If I then, your Lord and Teacher, have washed your feet, you also ought to wash one another's feet. For I have given you an example, that you also should do as I have done to you. Truly, truly, I say to you, a servant is not greater than his master; nor is he who is sent greater than he who sent him. If you know these things, blessed are you if you do them."

After that, Jesus was visibly troubled. He said, "Truly, I say to you, one of you will betray me." Of course, they all denied it and they looked at each other with suspicion. Just imagine the pain that caused Jesus, knowing that a dear friend would betray him. Have you ever had a friend break your trust? Have you been betrayed by a person you love? It hurts, doesn't it? Judas' betrayal hurt Jesus.

His heart was heavy, so heavy, after he spoke of Judas' betrayal. He did what he usually did when his heart was burdened, he went off to pray. This time he chose the Garden of Gethsemane as the place to go and commune with God. He took his disciples with him, but do you know what they did when he asked them to stay awake and pray with him? They fell asleep. They abandoned him. While Jesus fell to the ground, pouring out his heart and soul to God, his closest friends fell asleep. When he needed them the most, his disciples let him down.

I wish I would have been there with him. There were many nights that I had stayed awake with him, listening to his troubles, comforting his sorrows, and tending to his illnesses. I would have stayed awake with him. I, as his mother, would not have left him alone at such a time. But, not the disciples, they let him down. Three times Jesus asked, three times he asked them to stay awake, but they did not. The only comfort that I found was that God was with him. He prayed that God would take the cup, the cup of suffering and death, from him. As Jesus listened to God he learned that it was God's will that he go through with it and that God would be with him. That is what gave Jesus the strength to get up and meet his fate.

With Judas' kiss as a sign, the soldiers seized Jesus and took him away like a common criminal. Imagine my boy, who never hurt anyone, was dragged away like a murderer.

The disciples' betrayal and abandonment were enough for Jesus to bear, but on top of that one of his closest disciples denied him. Peter was hiding in the shadows as they took Jesus to the court of the high priest when three people asked him if he was one of Jesus' followers. Three times Peter denied knowing Jesus. The cock crowed and Peter cried, but I know that Jesus cried for him, too. Then they brought Jesus to Pilate. Pilate badgered him with questions, but Jesus said little. However, the crowd did not keep silent. The parade goers of Palm Sunday had a few things to say. It hurt me to see the fickleness of the crowd. Pilate said to the crowd, "What do you wish me to do with the man you call the King of the Jews?" The shouts of the Palm Sunday crowd changed from "Hosanna, hosanna" to "Crucify him. Crucify him." What kind of mixed message is that? My heart sank.

I would have gladly taken his place. I would have done anything to let my son go free and live. He had so much potential. But, as I looked in his eyes before they started flogging him, I knew he had to go through with it. His eyes said to me, "It is okay Mom. This is what I was sent here to do. It is okay. God is with me." That gave me some comfort, but when they started to flog him with the leather strap with steel spurs on the end if it, I thought I was going to die, too. Do you have any idea what it is like to watch your son be beaten until he goes limp?

I wish I could say that it ended there, but I cannot. They were not through with him yet. With the flesh of his back beaten raw, they made him carry his own cross until he could endure it no more. They gambled for his robe. I had made that robe myself. I wish they would have given it to me. I would have treasured it, but they used it as one more way to mock my son. Then they nailed him to the cross next to two thieves. While he was in excruciating pain, hanging from the spikes through his hands, he looked at me with great concern and said, "Mother, this is your son," as he pointed to John. John took me in and treated me as his own mother from that day on, but he never, never took the place of my son, Jesus.

That week was the worst week of my life as I watched Jesus go through all that he endured — the crowds giving him a hero's welcome only to turn on him — and then the emotional pain of his friends betraying, abandoning, and denying him. The torment of his captors mocking and the physical pain of the beating and crucifixion was more than I could bear. I just knew that I could not go on without him. My world came to a screeching halt the day the Palm Sunday parade ended at the cross. The Pharisees, Sadducees, the fickle crowd, Pontius Pilate, and the Roman soldiers thought they had the last word, but they did not. God did. When God raised my son from the dead, God had the last word and it was a word of victory. My son lives. Jesus lives. His death was for a reason. Jesus died so that nothing can bring our world to a screeching halt. "Hosanna, hosanna. Blessed is he who comes in the name of the Lord. Hosanna in the highest."

Listen to the words of a mother who is shocked at the words uttered by an old man at the time of her son's circumcision. What did Simeon mean when he looked at Mary, the mother of Jesus, and said, "A sword will pierce through your own soul"? Mary learns the true sense of what this man predicted as she encounters Jesus at different times throughout his life. Her soul is pierced, because his life is given — for her!

A Piercing Word
John 19:1-28

I often reflect back to the day when I met Simeon, the old, old man in the temple who sang God's praises the day we brought Jesus into the temple for circumcision. He took my little boy in his arms and said, "Lord, now let thou thy servant depart in peace according to thy word; for mine eyes have seen thy salvation which thou hast prepared in the presence of all peoples, a light for revelation to the Gentiles, and for glory to thy people Israel." Then he turned to me and said, "And a sword will pierce through your own soul also." I had no idea what that meant but I thought about those words often.

The first time those words came back to me was when we had to flee for the life of our young child. Herod, in a jealous rage, ordered that all the Hebrew boys under the age of two be killed. You see, he had heard from the men that had followed a star to Bethlehem that a king was born and he wanted to be assured that no one would take away his power and glory. In order to save our toddler's life we fled to Egypt. We stayed exiled in Egypt until we heard that the wicked Herod was dead. My soul was pierced with fear and sadness when we had to run for our lives leaving family and friends behind.

Simeon's words came to mind again when Jesus was lost for several days. We had journeyed to Jerusalem for the Passover along with thousands of religious pilgrims. After the feast was over, we caravanned home with family and friends. We had not seen Jesus in our large group of traveling companions, but we did not think anything of it. We assumed that he was playing with other children his age until it was nightfall and we could not find him. We asked all of our kinsfolk and acquaintances and no one had seen him. Can you imagine my panic when I realized that he was gone? I was worried sick. It seemed that we were traveling in slow motion as we headed back to Jerusalem. My mind was racing. Of course, I assumed the worst. I thought I would never see my precious son again. Joseph tried to reassure me, but that was fruitless. For three days, for three hopeless days, we scoured the city. We retraced our steps and then retraced them again.

When we found him I wanted to hug him and shake him all at the same time. I wanted to scream, "Do you know what you put me through?" But, I didn't, because when we found him, in the temple of all places, my anger gave way to relief. We found our twelve-year-old son in the temple studying scriptures with the elders. When I told him how worried I had been, the only thing he said was, "This is where I belong, in my Father's house." Can you imagine? He was only twelve years old! Most twelve-year-old boys need to be dragged to the temple. Not my son! He loved the temple. He considered it his home.

I also remember the time when Jesus had just begun his public ministry and he came back to our hometown. The people, even some of our neighbors that had known him since he was a boy, got so upset at his teachings that they nearly pushed him off a cliff. My soul was pierced as Jesus felt such fierce rejection from our friends and neighbors.

Oh, there were many, many times that I reflected back on Simeon's words. But, it was not until the day that my son was taken before the high priests and Pilate that I really knew what he meant. It was not until I heard the crowd shout, "Crucify him! Crucify him," that I really felt a sword pierce my soul.

I really could not believe it. Jesus had done nothing, absolutely nothing, to deserve that kind of treatment. Is that what you get when you treat people with dignity and love them uncondition-ally? Is that what people do when you cure the sick, give sight to the blind, and let the lame walk?

The sword pierced my heart with each cry of "crucify him." I felt so helpless. I wanted to run up to him and throw my arms around him to protect him like a mother hen covers her chicks with her wings. I wanted to beg them to stop. I wanted to plead with them to take me instead. But I merely stood there, frozen, stunned in disbelief.

My hope soared when Pilate said, "This man has done nothing wrong." I remember thinking that maybe Pilate was a man who understood my son. I was convinced that he saw the good in Jesus and I hoped that Pilate would do the right thing. However, my hopes waned when Pilate said, "It is my custom to release one prisoner. Who will it be? Jesus or Barabbas?" I thought certainly the crowd would not want Barabbas, a dangerous criminal, back on the streets. However, my hope faded and I knew the end was near when they yelled, "Give us Barabbas."

Before Pilate released Jesus into the hands of our Jewish leaders, to be crucified, he ordered my son to be flogged. That is something a mother should never have to endure. No mother should see her child tortured in such a way. Flogging is so cruel. They whipped my son with a leather strap that had metal barbs at the end. The barbs tore his flesh with each stroke. Each crack of the whip tore my heart. By the time they were done, his back was raw. Blood poured out of his exposed flesh. I wish I could have bound his wounds, but instead the soldiers mocked him by throwing a purple robe on his bleeding back. Can you imagine how that would have hurt? It brings me to tears just thinking about it.

One soldier placed a crown of thorns on his head while others struck him. I knew exactly what Simeon meant when I heard their mocking torment of "Hail, King of the Jews."

I could tell that Jesus was in excruciating pain, but they made him walk to Golgotha carrying his own cross. When he fell to his knees in pain, they forced him back to his feet. My knees went weak. I could barely stand, but John, a dear friend of my son, helped me along. As we arrived at Golgotha, I did not know how he could endure another minute, but he had a look of determination on his face. It was the same look he had at age twelve when we found him in the temple. That determined face said to me, "Mom, this is where I need to be. This is what I have to do." I took comfort in that familiar look I saw in his eyes.

However, that look changed to sheer terror when they threw his flesh-torn back against the cross. One soldier grabbed his wrists and another soldier took his legs. Then they drove a heavy iron spike through his wrists and through his feet. With each pound of the spike, my body shuttered in horror. I felt ill as I watched. I tried to run up and stop them, but John and another disciple held me back. They were worried what the ruthless soldiers would do to me.

They ... crucified ... my ... son ... my ... Jesus.

As he hung there in excruciating pain, I wondered where God was. Where was this God of love I had heard Jesus talk about so many times? Where was God when my son needed God the most? My son loved God more than anything, but where was God?

I felt terrible about questioning God at such a time. It was as if my son knew what I was thinking when he asked, "My God, my God, why have you forsaken me?" Then my questions did not seem so wrong. If Jesus could ask them, so could I.

I fell to my knees and wept. I cried uncontrollably. There was nothing else I could do. I knew the end was coming. I could not bear it. His breathing was labored. His suffering was palpable. He was suffocating. My son was dying while I helplessly watched. It was devastating. It did not feel like my soul was being pierced, it felt like my soul was being ripped apart. What would I do without my son? How can a mother live with such grief? How could I possibly go on? It is not the natural order of things. A mother should not watch her young son die.

Suddenly, I heard him speak to me. I don't know how he had the energy to say anything. Despite the torture, the pain, and the agony, as he hung there fighting for every breath, my son was thinking about me. He pointed to John and said, "Woman, behold your son." And to John he said, "Behold, your mother." Even in the throes of death he was watching out for me, his mom. He created family for me. He gave John and me to the care and keeping of each other. John could never replace the son that I was losing, no one could, but it helped to know that I would not be alone in my grief.

You don't know how many times those words of loving concern have played over and over again in my mind. Those last words that I heard my son say to me have brought me comfort in the midst of my incredible sorrow.

But, what has been most comforting to me was knowing that what happened to my son was not in vain. His excruciating, painful death was for a reason. That reason was you and me. He died so that we might live life abundantly now and forever. My son did not die in vain; he died for the love of the whole world. He died for the love of us. He died for the love of me and you.